I have Anxiety

By: Angela Samson

Illustrated by: Lubna Almousa

This book is dedicated to

My amazing parents Wanda and Russell Priest who have always loved, supported and shown me there›s nothing I cannot do.

My incredible husband Jesse Samson who is my perfect partner, and has always loved, helped and supported me through everything.

To our two amazing children William and Callie Samson who make every single day magical, wonderful and an adventure. They gave me the greatest gift in the whole world getting to be their mom.

To my friends and family who read my book many times before this point and pushed with love and encouragement that I could get it made into a real book. To my amazing Illustrator who did a perfect job bringing my story to life. And to the readers who have been struggling or have a child struggling from an Anxiety Disorder. This book is dedicated to you in hopes it can help you understand your Anxiety Disorder better. Remember you're not alone, your feelings and symptoms are real, and when you learn to manage your symptoms and you will, you can do anything!

- Angela Samson

Hi, my name is Angela, and I have an Anxiety Disorder.

When I was smaller, sometimes I would feel overwhelmed or mad, even when nothing was wrong.

Sometimes I would feel sad and want to cry, even when nothing was sad.

Sometimes I would feel sick or like I had a tummy bug, but then it would just pass.

My parents took me to our doctor. After talking to our doctor and him running some tests, he told me I have something called an Anxiety Disorder. He said it was REAL! Boy, did that make me feel better.

The doctor sent me to a special doctor called a Psychologist.
She helps me with my Anxiety Disorder.
She's another important person on my team.

An Anxiety Disorder means that my brain processes my feelings and situations differently than some people.

It's ok that my normal is different.
Just because it's different doesn't mean it's bad. It's also kind of like a super power, I know my feelings and myself really well because of my Anxiety Disorder.

People of all ages have Anxiety Disorders. From kids very small, all the way up to grown ups.

I don't always know what causes my Anxiety symptoms.
But that's ok, my symptoms don't always need a reason.
It's just important I know how to make my symptoms better.

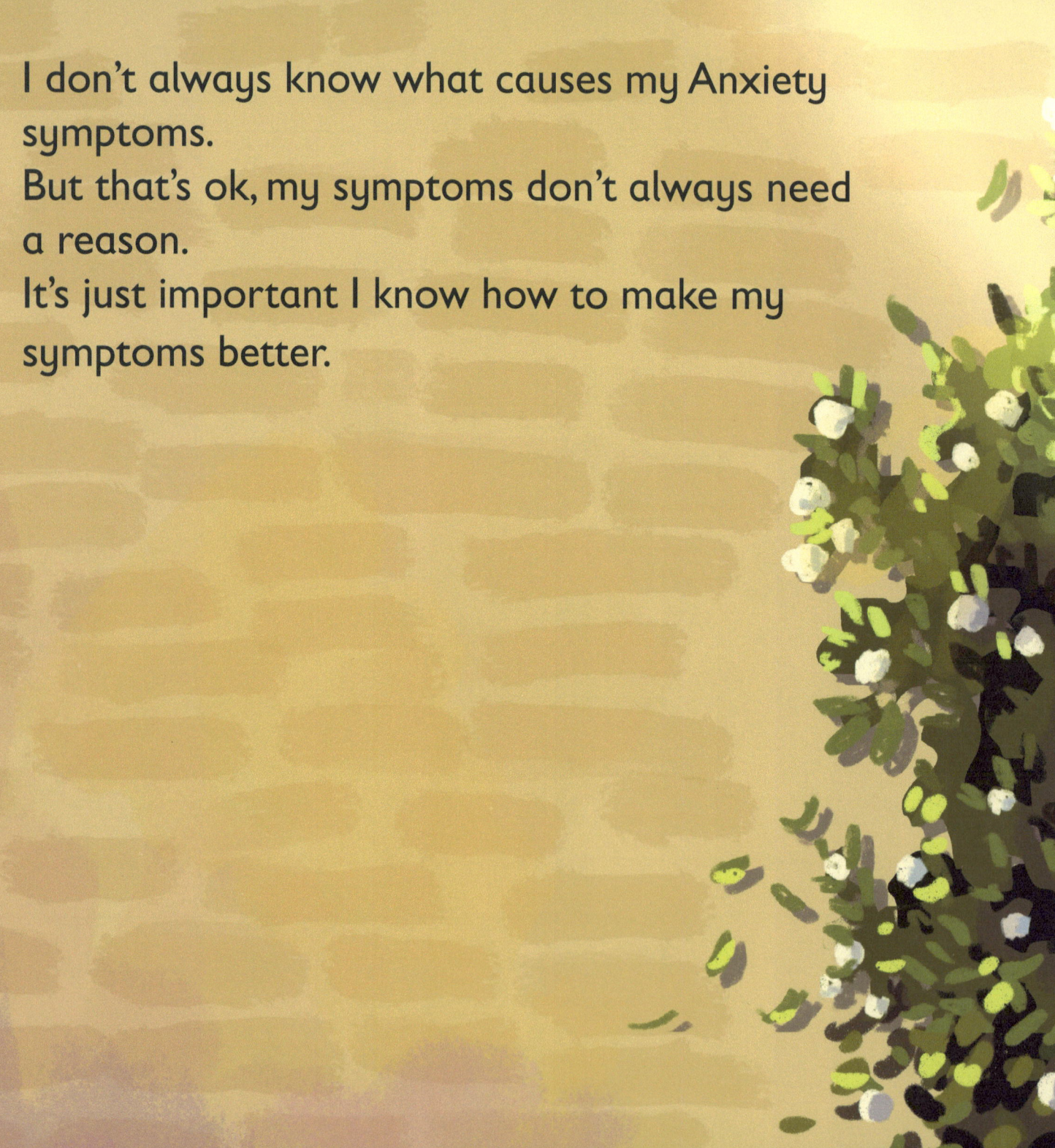

My feelings are very real. I can't make my symptoms go away, they are part of my Anxiety Disorder.
But I've learned things that can help me understand my Anxiety better.
There's things I can do to help control my Anxiety Disorder and not let it control me.

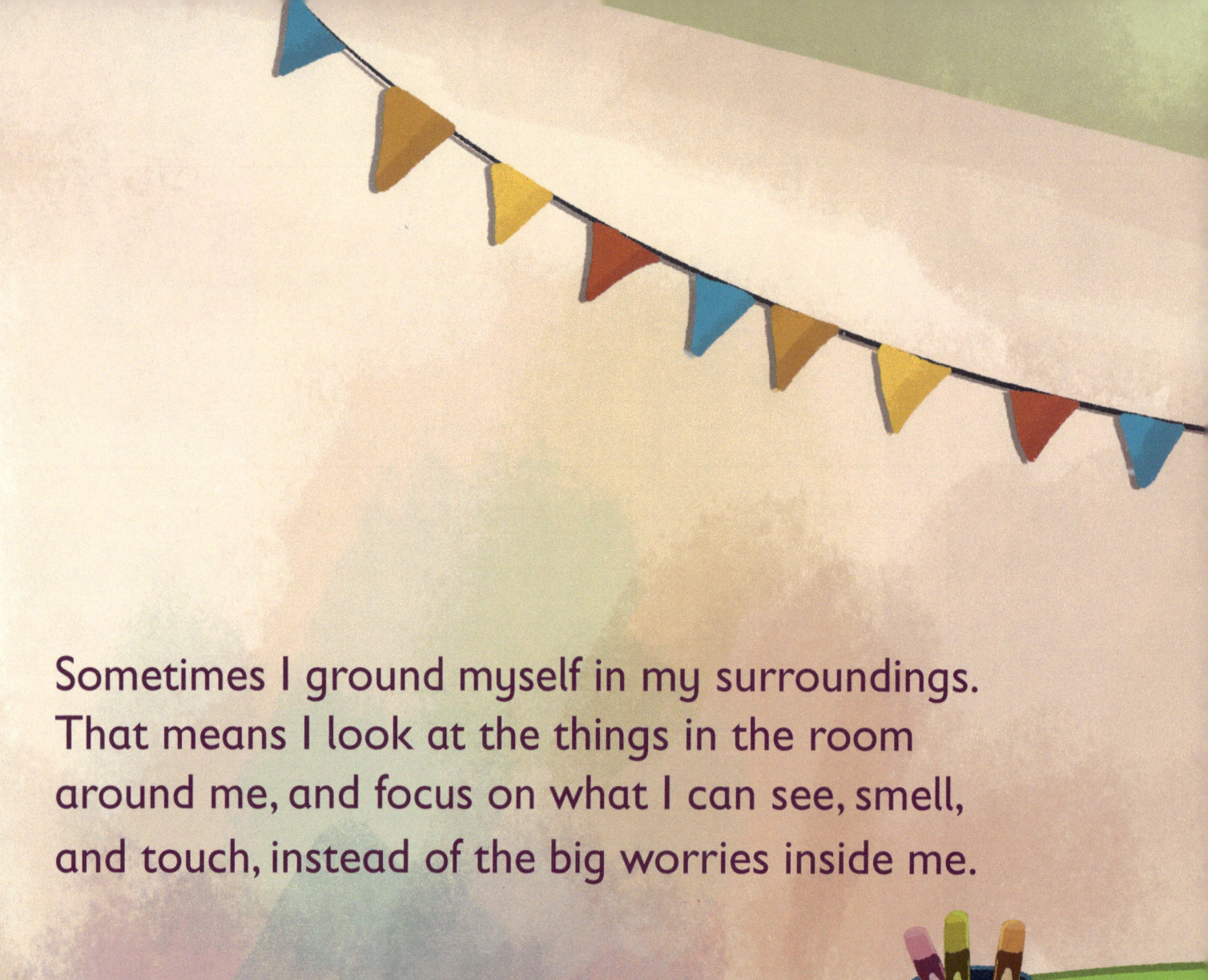

Sometimes I ground myself in my surroundings. That means I look at the things in the room around me, and focus on what I can see, smell, and touch, instead of the big worries inside me.

1

Sometimes I take
BIIIIIIIIG deep breaths

2

3

4

And blow out the worries from way deep in my belly.

Sometimes it helps to take a walk outside with my parents, and get some fresh air.

I have something called a **worry bag**. Inside it I take things with me that help me feel better.
It has:
books, colouring books, crayons, and a soft teddy bear to help when things feel too much and I need
a distraction.
Everyone's worry bag looks different.

The biggest thing I've learned is to talk to my mom, dad, doctor, and all the people around me who love me.
It's very important to talk about how I'm feeling even when I'm not sure exactly **what my feelings are.**

Even though my Anxiety can feel scary and confusing, when I talk about my feelings it can help.

Anxiety can feel very big sometimes,
but the love of my family and friends is bigger.

Angela Samson is an author from rural Nova Scotia, Canada. She grew up with two amazing parents who inspired her to imagine, be creative, and passed on a love of books and words.

Angela has always loved to write. She was a Daycare Teacher for years and had the opportunity to teach many children with Anxiety Disorders. She also has a certificate from New Skills in Child Psychology, and had her own diagnosis of a Childhood Anxiety Disorder and Panic Attack Disorder. All of these things really showed her how important talking about Childhood Anxiety Disorders are.

She now lives in her little home in the country with her incredible husband, two absolutely amazing children, and their adorable pets making everyday a magical, wonderful adventure.

www.ingramcontent.com/pod-product-compliance
Lightning Source LLC
Chambersburg PA
CBHW042248100526
44587CB00002B/67